Truth Be Told

amanda l hawkins

For those that
are broken with
truth waiting to
be told

this poetry
prompt book
will help you
find healing

and a voice

When working on a prompt, take your time. Think about what is being asked and let it flow. If you start to lose focus while writing, keep going! Once you're done, reread what you wrote and underline the most important lines. The best poems come from letting it all out. If the prompt doesn't apply to you, but it inspires you to write something else, do so! Just make sure that your work is coming out natural. Don't force yourself to write if it isn't work that you would like to share. These prompts aren't tended to be written in order so go crazy and pick from the 365 poetry prompts! Remain with an open mind and an open heart. Greatness WILL come out of this.

If you'd like to show me your work that has come from any these prompts, email me!

amandalhawkins7@gmail.com

PROMPT #1

What do you feel in
this exact moment?

PROMPT #2

What do you find
most beautiful about
people?

PROMPT #3

Your pillow has heard your
thoughts. What would it
say back to you if it could?

PROMPT #4

Use the word "alive"
in your poem.

PROMPT #5

Who can put butterflies
in your stomach?

PROMPT #6

Compare yourself to
a source of light.

PROMPT #7

Write a poem about
running low on energy.

PROMPT #8

Use the word "remedy"
in your poem.

PROMPT #9

Is your intuition
usually correct? Write
about it.

PROMPT #10

What has been your
biggest stepping
stone?

PROMPT #11

Explain why it's hard to
listen to your heart and
mind at the same time.

PROMPT #12

Write a poem about
the scent of rain.

PROMPT #13

Has your life been more
positive? Or negative?

PROMPT #14

Write a poem about
your hands.

PROMPT #15

"no amount of money"

PROMPT #16

Write a poem about
a caged bird.

PROMPT #17

Dedicate a poem to
someone.

PROMPT #18

Compare someone in
your life as a shield.

PROMPT #19

Write about not having a
care in the world.

PROMPT #20

Write about loving the
wrong person.

PROMPT #21

Use the word "heavy" in
your poem.

PROMPT #22

Write about a dream that
you didn't want to wake
up from.

PROMPT #23

Pick a person you care
about and write about
their eyes.

PROMPT #24

Write a poem about a
monster.

PROMPT #25

Say "help me"
somewhere in your
poem.

PROMPT #26

"you are...."

PROMPT #27

Write about the feeling of
walking in sand.

PROMPT #28

Start your poem with
"what if"

PROMPT #29

Find your favorite picture.
And write about it as if it
is currently happening.

PROMPT #30

What is a trait you wish
everyone had?

PROMPT #31

Write a poem describing
the last person you spoke
to without saying their
name.

PROMPT #32

Write about a
paintbrush.

PROMPT #33

What is something on your
bucket-list? Write about it.

PROMPT #34

"life goes fast when
you..." Finish the poem.

PROMPT #35

Does oblivion scare you?

PROMPT #36

Write a poem that is
motivational.

PROMPT #37

Go people-watching. Pick a
person and write about
what you think is going
through their head.

PROMPT #38

Your happiest memory.

PROMPT #39

What does hope look
like to you?

PROMPT #40

If you wanted an
adrenaline rush, where
would you go to get it?

PROMPT #41

Think about something
that takes up most of your
heart. Would you tell it to
stay? Or leave?

PROMPT #42

Compare your lover to an
article of clothing you
have.

PROMPT #43

Write a poem about going
backwards.

PROMPT #44

Write about a dried up
lake.

PROMPT #45

Write a poem about not
having shade.

PROMPT #46

Write about getting lost in a maze

PROMPT #47

"proceed with caution"

PROMPT #48

Write a poem about a
paper airplane.

PROMPT #49

How do you feel most
confident?

PROMPT #50

Compare life to a roller
coaster?

PROMPT #51

What were you told as a
child that isn't the same
now that you're older?

PROMPT #52

Write about something
running through your hair.

PROMPT #53

Vent.

PROMPT #54

Write a poem about a
special connection you
have with someone.

PROMPT #55

"it just happened"

PROMPT #56

Include the word
"suspicion" in your
poem.

PROMPT #57

Write a poem about a seed
that hasn't sprouted yet.

PROMPT #58

"like a baby"

PROMPT #59

Write about something you love and hate at the same time.

PROMPT #60

Write a poem about
something that is
permanent in your life.

PROMPT #61

Write a poem about a
knife.

PROMPT #62

A haunted house.

PROMPT #63

Find a birthmark on your
body and write about it.

PROMPT #64

Write about what gets you
out of your dark place.

PROMPT #65

In your mind, make a big
garden. Then write about
each section of this garden
as it applies to your life.

PROMPT #66

Write about looking
towards the sun.

PROMPT #67

What is your depression?

PROMPT #68

Write a poem about your
veins.

PROMPT #69

Compare yourself to a puzzle.

PROMPT #70

Do you have any self-doubt?

PROMPT #71

Describe the word
"temptation" in a poem.

PROMPT #72

Write a poem about being
blind.

PROMPT #73

Compare your younger self
to your older self. What
has changed?

PROMPT #74

Write a spoken word about
something that is on your
mind right now.

PROMPT #75

To be in the moment.

PROMPT #76

Express the word "kill" in
any way that you want.

PROMPT #77

Include the word "smoke"
in your poem.

PROMPT #78

Write about being the last
puppy in the box.

PROMPT #79

Write about moving
forward even with the odds
against you.

PROMPT #80

Write about boiling water.

PROMPT #81

"I'm running away"

PROMPT #82

Write about the wind.

PROMPT #83

A guilty pleasure.

PROMPT #84

What happens to you when
you see the one you love?

PROMPT #85

You know yourself more
than anyone else in this
world. What is your best
self-discovery?

PROMPT #86

A skyscraper.

PROMPT #87

Write a poem with the
word "temple".

PROMPT #88

Compare yourself to a
book.

PROMPT #89

What is your calling to this world?

PROMPT #90

Write about feeding a fire.

PROMPT #91

Write a poem about a
person that has taught you
the most lessons.

PROMPT #92

What is a lie you've told?

PROMPT #93

Write something that
rhymes.

PROMPT #94

Include the word "unfair"
in your poem.

PROMPT #95

Start with "I'm leaving".

PROMPT #96

Write about breaking glass.

PROMPT #97

A reason to exist.

PROMPT #98

Compare yourself to the
battery percentage on your
phone.

PROMPT #99

Two people fighting.

PROMPT #100

Write a poem about a deck
of cards.

PROMPT #101

What happens to you when
you cannot focus?

PROMPT #102

End your poem with "as I thought".

PROMPT #103

Write about the
neighborhood you grew
up in.

PROMPT #104

A rock skipping water.

PROMPT #105

Playing mind games.

PROMPT #106

Write about a dandelion.

PROMPT #107

While going through
situations in your life, how
do you remain whole?

PROMPT #108

What is something you
haven't seen in a long
time?

PROMPT #109

Write about the word
"survival".

PROMPT #110

Write a poem about
"crossing paths".

PROMPT #111

Write a text that you will
never send.

PROMPT #112

What is your earliest
memory?

PROMPT #113

Karma is a real person.
Who would you tell her to
get and why? Write this
poem without saying the
name of the person.

PROMPT #114

What is the best gift you
have ever received?

PROMPT #115

Write a poem about being
deaf.

PROMPT #116

Is it hard for you to fall
asleep?

PROMPT #117

Giving chances to someone.

PROMPT #118

What does your laugh
sound like?

PROMPT #119

What does your reflection
look like?

PROMPT #120

Write a poem about a tree
that doesn't have any
leaves.

PROMPT #121

What is your common
daydream?

PROMPT #122

Are you a day person or a
night person?

PROMPT #123

Write a poem of your daily
routine.

PROMPT #124

Does change scare you?

PROMPT #125

Write a poem about a
symbol that inspires you.

PROMPT #126

Start your poem with
"how could you".

PROMPT #127

Write a poem about a love
that isn't yours.

PROMPT #128

You're lost in a foreign
city.

PROMPT #129

Compare love to something
in your toolbox.

PROMPT #130

A dying fire.

PROMPT #131

Write a poem about
crawling.

PROMPT# 132

Write a poem about your
mother.

PROMPT #133

Write about how actions
speak louder than words.

PROMPT #134

You're stuck in a hole.

PROMPT #135

Write a poem about giving
yourself a break.

PROMPT #136

Write a poem about the
moon.

PROMPT #137

Write a paragraph about
learning something for the
first time.

PROMPT #138

"It's hard to breathe".

PROMPT #139

Compare yourself to a star
in the night sky.

PROMPT #140

Write a poem about your
father.

PROMPT #141

Making your heart a home.

PROMPT #142

Write a poem about
walking.

PROMPT #143

Include the words "so much" in your poem.

PROMPT #144

What are some "red flags"
to look for?

PROMPT #145

Write about something that
you can't forget even if
you tried.

PROMPT #146

Write about alcohol.

PROMPT #147

A feather from a bird.

PROMPT #148

Write about the fog that
will soon clear up.

PROMPT #149

Two people kissing.

PROMPT #150

What is the most valuable
lesson you have ever
learned?

PROMPT #151

In a creative way, write a
poem about what your
heart is made out of.

PROMPT #152

What is heaven to you?

PROMPT #153

What makes you angry the
most?

PROMPT #154

What is a risk you are
willing to take?

PROMPT #155

What made you turn into a savage?

PROMPT #156

"Love is..."

PROMPT #157

How does your love story
end?

PROMPT #158

Write a six word poem.

PROMPT #159

Hate.

PROMPT #160

Write a poem about being
youthful.

PROMPT #161

Compare sand to time
slipping away.

PROMPT #162

Write a letter to a child.

PROMPT #163

No one understanding.

PROMPT #164

Write a poem about
making a choice between
two really hard options.

PROMPT #165

Write a poem about a
soldier going to war.

PROMPT #166

Compare yourself to a
magic trick.

PROMPT #167

Write about a dice.

PROMPT #168

Staying in bed all day.

PROMPT #169

Something running
through your hair.

PROMPT #170

End your poem with
"I'm only human".

PROMPT #171

You're a passenger on a
train.

PROMPT #172

Write a poem about
floating in water.

PROMT #173

Write a poem about sitting
under the shade of a tree.

PROMPT #174

Write about running.

PROMPT #175

Write a poem about your
finish line.

PROMPT #176

Include the word
"confusion" in your poem.

PROMPT #177

What makes you feel brand new?

PROMPT #178

Write about beach waves.

PROMPT #179

What is an event that is
coming up in your life?
Write about it.

PROMPT #180

In this moment, what do
you want?

PROMPT #181

Write about what you think
the world would be like
without electronics.

PROMPT #182

Falling apart.

PROMPT #183

Falling together.

PROMPT #184

Start your rant with
"correct me if I am
wrong".

PROMPT #185

Write the instructions on
how you want to be loved.

PROMPT #186

You're an art piece in a
museum. What is one thing
you want everyone to
understand?

PROMPT #187

Rewrite something that
you've already wrote.

PROMPT #188

How did you meet your
lover?

PROMPT #189

Write about how you
cannot see clearly.

PROMPT #190

Write a poem that you
would make into a tattoo.

PROMPT #191

Write about being mute.

PROMPT #192

What is something that is
missing in your life?

PROMPT #193

A fear of not being enough.

PROMPT #194

If you could be an animal,
what would you be?

PROMPT #195

Write about a lie you
believed in.

PROMPT #196

Make a poem with made-
up words.

PROMPT #197

You're invisible.

PROMPT #198

Compare yourself to a
river.

PROMPT #199

Write about biting off more
than you can chew.

PROMPT #200

Write a poem about a wall.

PROMPT #201

Write a poem about an
object that is in your trash
right now.

PROMPT #202

What color best describes
you as a person?

PROMPT #203

Think about something
reckless you did in your
past. Do you regret it
today?

PROMPT #204

Compare a messy room to
a messy heart.

PROMPT #205

Write about a pain that
was caused by a family
member.

PROMPT #206

Write a poem about money.

PROMPT #207

Where does your strength
come from?

PROMPT #208

Write about a body weight
scale.

PROMPT #209

Write about what goes
through your head when
you choke on your words.

PROMPT #210

What is something that
you've done really nice for
someone?

PROMPT #211

Write about something that
you ignore.

PROMPT #212

Write about the word
"compromise".

PROMPT #213

Compare yourself to your
favorite drink.

PROMPT #214

Write about a time you
were rejected.

PROMPT #215

Write about something that
turns ugly over time.

PROMPT #216

Start your poem with "I
know it's hard but..."

PROMPT #217

Find an art piece that
speaks to you. Write about
it.

PROMPT #218

Compare yourself to a
raindrop.

PROMPT #219

Compare a damaged
blanket to a damaged
relationship.

PROMPT #220

Write a short story.

PROMPT #221

Write about addiction.

PROMPT #222

Do you like being alone?

PROMPT #223

An unforgettable
experience.

PROMPT #224

Who was the first person
to show you what a
heartbreak was?

PROMPT #225

A hard shell to crack.

PROMPT #226

Write about a tattoo that
you have. Or one that you
would get.

PROMPT #227

Use the word "rise" in
your poem.

PROMPT #228

Write a poem about a piece
of mail you have received.

PROMPT #229

Ask an elder what they
wish they had known
growing up.

PROMPT #230

Write a poem about a
promise you have broken.

PROMPT #231

If you had wings, where
would you fly?

PROMPT #232

Write about a time you felt
left out.

PROMPT #233

Describe a road trip you've
been on.

PROMPT #234

Start your poem with
"maybe in another life".

PROMPT #235

If one of your wounds
could talk, what would it
say?

PROMPT #236

Compare being "stood up"
to something.

PROMPT #237

What mind would you want
to live in for a day?

PROMPT #238

What do you regret the most?

PROMPT #239

Who is someone that
makes you forget to
breathe?

PROMPT #240

Say "thank you" to
someone.

PROMPT #241

What do you need more of
in your life?

PROMPT #242

Write a sexy poem.

PROMPT #243

How do you heal from a
heartbreak?

PROMPT #244

Compare yourself to a
volcano. Are you calm or
ready to explode?

PROMPT #245

Write a poem about the
word "stealing".

PROMPT #246

Write about a good hiding
spot.

PROMPT #247

Having the eyes of a baby.

PROMPT #248

Write a poem about
something getting cold with
time.

PROMPT #249

Go to the beach and get the most unique shell you can find. Write about it.

PROMPT #250

Write about a planet. Make
sure to use their
characteristics.

PROMPT #251

A cut down tree.

PROMPT #252

"No one will stop me"

PROMPT #253

Write about a bookshelf.

PROMPT #254

Write a poem about life
passing by slowly.

PROMPT #255

Who or what energizes you?

PROMPT #256

What does you handwriting
say about you?

PROMPT #257

Have you ever broke
anything out of anger?

PROMPT #258

Wiping tears.

PROMPT #259

Write a poem about your
fingers touching something
smooth.

PROMPT #260

What do you think about
when all the windows are
down while you drive?

PROMPT #261

Write a poem of a question
you have and the answer.

PROMPT #262

If you had to be a season,
which season would you
be?

PROMPT #263

Think about a time you got
hurt physically. Write
about it.

PROMPT #264

Write about strength.

PROMPT #265

Compare love to an
instrument.

PROMPT #266

Is it hard for you to take
your own advice?

PROMPT #267

"I learned the hard way"

PROMPT #268

Who is your favorite
notification?

PROMPT #269

What is a dream that you
had in the past and still
remember?

PROMPT #270

Write a poem of a birds
view looking down on the
earth.

PROMPT #271

Write a poem about lust
without saying the word
lust.

PROMPT #272

Your heart is a door. Who
has the key?

PROMPT #273

What does happiness taste
like to you?

PROMPT #274

Your name is a beautiful
thing. Write a poem with
the letters of it.

PROMPT #275

Write a poem with the
perspective of a stray dog.

PROMPT #276

Write about something that
you have made in the past.

PROMPT #277

Think about your favorite place. What does it smell like?

PROMPT #278

Write about the time it is
for you right now.

PROMPT #279

Compare yourself to an
unraveling sweater.

PROMPT #280

Express your current pain.

PROMPT #281

Write about the word
"unconditional".

PROMPT #282

What do you do when you
need your mind to calm?

PROMPT #283

What is a nightmare that
you remember having?

PROMPT #284

Do you think that your
zodiac sign and your
personality match?

PROMPT #285

Time stood still.

PROMPT #286

Write about your
bedsheets.

PROMPT #287

Write about how hard to is
to let go of something that
you love so much.

PROMPT #288

Write a poem off of a
recent phone call you have
had with someone.

PROMPT #289

Go to your photo gallery
and write about the oldest
picture taken.

PROMPT #290

Get a newspaper and write
about something that is
currently happening.

PROMPT #291

If you could make a potion,
what would this potion do?

PROMPT #292

Go on social media and
write about a picture you
see.

PROMPT #293

Write a poem about two
things that are opposite
from each other.

PROMPT #294

Reincarnation.

PROMPT #295

Compare mechanical issues
with a body part.

PROMPT #296

Write about a specific
object you've held onto for
a long time.

PROMPT #297

Write about searching for
something that has been
hiding from you.

PROMPT #298

Write about how it isn't
always greener on the
other side.

PROMPT #299

What is the hardest thing
you've ever had to do?

PROMPT #300

What does your soul look like?

PROMPT #301

How does your love story
start?

PROMPT #302

Start with "I wish.."

PROMPT #303

You have up to 20 words
to make a difference. what
do you say?

PROMPT #304

Compare a person to a
crumbled piece of paper.

PROMPT #305

Write a poem off of a text
that you have on your
phone.

PROMPT #306

Write about yourself.

PROMPT #307

The magic you see in them.

PROMPT #308

What is the key to happiness?

PROMPT #309

What does your name
mean? Is it accurate to
your personality?

PROMPT #310

Write a poem about holding
hands.

PROMPT #311

Who or what is your
kryptonite?

PROMPT #312

Think about your best
characteristic. How would
you use this trait as an
evil power?

PROMPT #313

Is there something that
you hate about yourself?
Write about it as if you
loved it.

PROMPT #314

What is your biggest
insecurity?

PROMPT #315

Write about the last time
that you shown yourself
some love.

PROMPT #316

"I love you but..."
Finish the sentence.

PROMPT #317

Have you expressed your
feelings towards someone?
Write about their reaction.

PROMPT #318

Start with "no..."

PROMPT #319

What would you say to
your mirror right now?

PROMPT #320

Compare your body to a
body of water.

PROMPT #321

Why aren't your white
shoes white anymore?

PROMPT #322

What do you think your
haters will say when you
achieve your goal?

PROMPT #323

Your soul is waiting on an apology. What would it be about?

PROMPT #324

Sit where you feel most
comfortable and write
about an object that is in
the room.

PROMPT #325

If you had a seed to grow
anything under the sun,
what would it be?

PROMPT #326

A fake smile.

PROMPT #327

Quick! What is the first
thing that pops in your
head?

PROMPT #328

What would your house
look like without love?

PROMPT #329

What is your 'zodiac
reading of the day'? Is it
accurate?

PROMPT #330

An empty picture frame.

PROMPT #331

What is something that
you want to know but
scared to know the
answer?

PROMPT #332

Imagine meeting yourself
through someone else's
eyes. What would your
first impression be?

PROMPT #333

Write about what you see
out the window.

PROMPT #334

They say that your worst
fear in your life is how you
died in your past life. How
did you die?

PROMPT #335

Look at the clouds. What is
the first thing that comes
to mind?

PROMPT #336

If your heart needed a
rest. Where would it lay?

PROMPT #337

You're a flower that has
been picked off the ground.
What do you say to the
picker?

PROMPT #338

Start your poem with
"let me".

PROMPT #339

With all the labels in this world, which label will you live by?

PROMPT #340

Think of an insult someone
has told you in the past.
Write about it.

PROMPT #341

Write about how it may
feel to sit on the edge of a
really tall building.

PROMPT #342

Put some instrumental
music on. While you listen,
take some deep breaths.
Write.

PROMPT #343

Write a poem that you will
eventually give a person
when the time is right.

PROMPT #344

If you were a place, where
would you be?

PROMPT #345

Open a dictionary to a
random page. Pick a word
and write about it.

PROMPT #346

What is your favorite
song? Write about the
message of the song.

PROMPT #347

Think about a fairytale
that you were told as a
child. Pick one and rewrite
it.

PROMPT #348

A broken clock.

PROMPT #349

Write about the sidewalks
you see everyday.

PROMPT #350

Muddy water.

PROMPT #351

They say that love gets
better with age. But I say
the younger the heart is,
the faster it beats. What do
you think?

PROMPT #352

You have the opportunity
to change the whole world.
Who are you helping first?

PROMPT #353

A sad kiss.

PROMPT #354

Include the word
"remember" in your poem.

PROMPT #355

If a shooting star crossed
you right now, what would
you wish for?

PROMPT #356

What is something that
you've learned recently
that has changed your
perspective on life?

PROMPT #357

Find a book that you have
and write about a sentence
that you come across.

PROMPT #358

Write about growing into
your own person.

PROMPT #359

Awake in the middle of the
night.

PROMPT #360

Let it out.

PROMPT #361

Write about your life in one
line increments.

PROMPT #362

Escape.

PROMPT #363

Put your music on shuffle
and write about the first
3-5 words you hear.

PROMPT #364

Include the word "carry" in
your poem.

PROMPT #365

Is your heart okay?